RISE ABOVE

Reclaim your life with a transformational mindset

Lawrence Badman

Welcome to Your Journey

In today's society, there is a growing openness around discussing mental health and personal challenges, with more people sharing how they feel and the obstacles they are striving to overcome. This shift towards vulnerability and self-awareness is paving the way for greater understanding and support. This book is designed to provide practical tools and insights to help you navigate these areas, empowering you to take control of your mindset and personal growth. What makes this journey even more impactful is that any profits from the book will be donated to a charity, so while you invest in your own development, you are also contributing to others who need the support that charity provides. Together, we can foster a culture of growth, understanding, and positive change.

About the book:

Each chapter focuses on a specific theme, offering insights, strategies, and exercises to help you explore and address these challenges in your life.

I have used the term 'men' throughout this book for ease of writing, but the principles and tools shared are designed to help both men and women overcome life's barriers.

How to Navigate the Book:
1. Read with an Open Mind
   Approach each chapter as an opportunity for self-reflection. Be open to new ideas, even if they feel unfamiliar or uncomfortable at first. Personal growth often begins outside of your comfort zone.
2. Take Your Time
   There is no rush to finish this eBook. Move at your own pace, allowing the ideas and concepts to sink in. The exercises are meant to help you reflect on your thoughts and experiences. Give yourself the space and time to complete them thoughtfully.

3. Engage with the Exercises

   Each chapter includes exercises designed to help you apply the concepts to your own life. To gain the most from these, treat them as a personal conversation between you and your mindset. Write down your answers honestly and use them as a tool to reflect on your current beliefs, feelings, and behaviours.
   - Action Step: After reading the chapter, set aside dedicated time to work through the exercises. Use a journal or a notes app to track your progress.

4. Reflect Deeply

   Reflection is key to transformation. Each exercise is followed by a reflection prompt. Take this as an opportunity to dive deeper into your thoughts, identifying patterns or roadblocks that are holding you back.
   - Action Step: Ask yourself, "How does this apply to me? How have I faced these challenges in the past, and what can I do differently moving forward?"

5. Set Goals and Intentions

   At the end of each chapter, consider setting a small,

achievable goal based on what you've learned. Whether it's reframing a negative thought or practicing self-compassion, setting intentions will solidify your progress.

6. Revisit and Rework

   Personal development is a continual process. As you move through this book, you may find it helpful to revisit chapters or exercises, especially as new challenges arise in your life. Reflect on how your mindset and approach have evolved over time.

7. Use the Call to Action

   Throughout the book, there are call-to-action moments where you'll be encouraged to pause, think, and take action. Whether it's performing a self-reflection exercise or making a plan for the week ahead, these are designed to help you put the concepts into practice immediately.

8. Embrace the Journey

   Progress may not always be linear. Celebrate your wins, no matter how small, and use setbacks as learning opportunities. Growth is a journey, and every step you take brings you closer to the best version of yourself

Acknowledgements

I would like to extend my deepest thanks to *The Coaching Masters* for the inspiration and support that set me on the path to writing this book. Their educational content and the wealth of supporting materials have had a profound impact on my outlook on life, challenging me to think differently and approach personal growth with renewed purpose. The lessons I've learned from their coaching programs have not only enriched my journey but have also played a key role in shaping the ideas within these pages. Thank you for empowering me to believe in the power of transformation.

About the author

I have been employed as a coach educator with the Football Association of Wales for over 17 years in a job that I love, supporting coaches to develop.

I am also a transformational mindset coach, author, and ICF-accredited master coach with a passion for empowering professional men to overcome barriers and achieve their full potential.

With a MSc in Performance Coaching, a BSc (Hons) in Applied Sports Science, a UEFA A coaching licence, and a UEFA football management qualification, I combine expertise in mindset development and performance enhancement to help clients unlock their personal and professional success. Drawing from years of experience, including overcoming personal challenges like health setbacks, self-doubt, and imposter syndrome, I am dedicated to helping others find clarity, confidence, and purpose in their lives and I hope this book will help the reader with any challenges they face.

Preface

On October 15th, 2021, my life took a sharp, unexpected turn. I collapsed at home and was rushed to the hospital, where I was diagnosed with a massive pulmonary embolism, brought on by COVID-19.

I spent the next week in hospital with four of those days in the high dependency unit. The doctor told me afterward that many people wouldn't have made it through. I realized then how close I came to not being here today.

That experience changed everything for me. Lying in that hospital bed, I had a lot of time to think about my life—what I was doing with it, and where I wanted to go. There was no escaping the reality that we all have a limited amount of time, and I had been given a second chance. It wasn't just about surviving anymore; it was about living with intention.

Since that day, my outlook on life has shifted. I no longer have the patience or energy for things that don't add value to my life. Whether that's relationships, hobbies, or even small daily habits, I've learned to focus only on what truly matters.

I want to be involved in things that inspire, challenge, and uplift me—and I want the same for other people who, like me, have faced their own struggles and are searching for more meaning and fulfilment.

This book is a product of that transformation. It's not just a collection of ideas but a roadmap based on my own journey of growth, self-discovery, and resilience. I've walked this path, and now I want to help other men walk it too. Life is too short to settle for anything less than a life that fuels your passion and purpose. This is the mindset that saved my life, and I believe it can transform yours as well.

Table of Contents

Introduction 1
Chapter 1: Building Confidence Unlocking Your Potential 5
Chapter 2: Growth Mindset vs. Fixed Mindset 13
Chapter 3: Resilience 23
Chapter 4: Breaking Free from Overthinking 32
Chapter 5: Overcoming Imposter Syndrome 42
Chapter 6: Breaking the Chains of Procrastination 52
Chapter 7: Overcoming Anxiety 58
Chapter 8: Overcoming Self-Sabotage 66
Chapter 9: Overcoming Dopamine Addiction 73
Chapter 10: Overcoming Fear 82
Chapter 11: Breaking Free from Validation 89
Chapter 12: Overcoming Lack of Self-Esteem 97
Chapter 13: Emotional Intelligence 105
Chapter 14: Overcoming Perfectionism 113
Conclusion: Embrace Your Journey 121

Introduction

Do you ever feel like you're not good enough, even when you've achieved success? Does self-doubt creep in, making you question your abilities, your worth, or your future? If so, you're not alone. Many men, despite their accomplishments, feel held back by invisible barriers: growth mindset, resilience, and a constant lack of confidence amongst other issues.

These feelings can create a cycle that traps you in place, no matter how much effort you put in. You push yourself to perform at your best, but inside, something feels off. You know you're capable of more, yet something inside keeps telling you otherwise.

This book is designed to help you break free from that trap. It's a guide for men like you—men who want more from life but feel stuck. Whether it's in your career, relationships, or personal development, the real obstacle isn't out there in the world. It's within. Your mindset holds the key.

My Story

I've been where you are now. There was a time in my life when I felt like I wasn't enough. Even after years of hard work, building a career, and achieving success, I was plagued by anxiety, imposter syndrome, and a deep sense of inadequacy. My health suffered, and I lacked the confidence to push myself forward.

Through this book, I'll share the lessons I learned, not just from my own struggles, but from working with countless men facing the same battles. Men who have learned to shift their mindset, redefine success, and unlock the confidence that had been buried deep within.

Why Your Mindset Matters

Your mindset isn't just one part of the equation—it's everything. It shapes how you react to challenges, how you manage setbacks, and ultimately, how far you go in life. With the right mindset, those barriers of doubt, fear, and uncertainty can be transformed into fuel for growth.

So, what would your life look like if you could conquer those doubts? What if anxiety and self-doubt no longer dictated your decisions? Imagine waking up each day with confidence, clarity, and a sense of purpose.

Your Journey Starts Here

But before we dive into strategies, I want to ask you to reflect on where you are today. Take a moment and honestly consider these questions:

1. What's the biggest mental hurdle you're dealing with right now?
2. How does anxiety or self-doubt affect your work, relationships, or personal goals?
3. What would change in your life if you could break free from the grip of imposter syndrome and low self-esteem?
4. What would it mean to feel confident every day, not just in moments of success, but even when things don't go according to plan?

Call to Action: Setting Your Intention

Here's your first step. Before moving forward, write down one goal you have for yourself. It can be anything—a shift in mindset, a career goal, or simply feeling more confident. Then ask yourself: **What's holding me back from achieving this?**

This is the beginning of your journey to unlocking your potential and becoming the man you were meant to be. By the time you finish this book, you'll have not only the tools to conquer your mental barriers, but also the clarity and strength to move forward with confidence.

Chapter 1

Building Confidence Unlocking Your Potential

Introduction

Confidence is the foundation of achieving personal and professional success. It is the belief in your ability to meet challenges head-on, make decisions, and take action without second-guessing yourself. Whether it's making a big career move, speaking in front of a crowd, or tackling a personal goal, confidence empowers you to push past fear and self-doubt. Yet, many people, especially in high-pressure roles, struggle with confidence, feeling unsure of their abilities or afraid of failure. In this chapter, we'll explore how lack of confidence shows up in your life, offer tools to help you build a resilient mindset, and guide you toward unleashing your full potential.

Lack of Confidence in Action

Lack of confidence doesn't just remain a mental block—it manifests in various aspects of life. It shows up when you procrastinate because you're afraid of making a mistake. It may stop you from speaking up in meetings, leading to missed opportunities, it can also lead you to feel as though you're being judged by significant others whenever you deliver any form of presentation, practical demonstration, or speech. This has happened to me on occasions and had a negative impact, just thinking about what the others were thinking about my delivery rather than being focused on the content I am delivering. However, people don't think as much about you, as you believe they do.

This lack of confidence can keep you from setting bold goals, leading to stagnation in your personal and professional growth. The effects of low confidence can be far-reaching, impacting not just your self-esteem, but also your relationships, career trajectory, and overall sense of well-being.

Common signs of lack of confidence include:

- **Self-Doubt:** Constant questioning of your abilities or decisions.
- **Perfectionism:** A fear of failure that leads to overthinking and avoidance of tasks.

- **Avoidance**: Steering clear of challenges or opportunities because of fear of not measuring up.
- **Negative Self-Talk**: Internal dialogue focused on what you can't do rather than what you can achieve.

The impact of these behaviours may not always be visible, but they slow down your progress and limit your potential. Overcoming lack of confidence is not about changing who you are—it's about reframing your mindset and unlocking your innate strengths

Interactive Quiz to Measure Your Level of Confidence

Take a moment to assess your current level of confidence by answering the following questions. Rate each on a scale of 1 to 5, where 1 = strongly disagree, 2 = disagree,

3 =neutral, 4 = agree and 5 = strongly agree.
1. I feel confident making decisions without second-guessing myself.
2. I take initiative in work and personal projects without waiting for others to lead.
3. I regularly set and achieve goals that push me outside my comfort zone.

4. I maintain a positive outlook even when faced with setbacks.
5. I believe I can handle challenges that come my way, no matter how difficult they seem.

Results:

- **15-25**: Low confidence – You might often second-guess yourself, avoid challenges, or feel overwhelmed by uncertainty.
- **26-35**: Moderate confidence – You have some belief in your abilities but could benefit from further strengthening your mindset to take on greater challenges.
- **36-45**: High confidence – You trust in your abilities, and you're ready to take bold steps toward success. There may still be occasional self-doubt, but it doesn't hold you back.

Tools to Support Overcoming Lack of Confidence

Building lasting confidence takes time and practice. Fortunately, there are tools and strategies you can implement to strengthen your mindset and shift away from self-doubt.

1. **Mindset Reframing:** Change the narrative you tell yourself. Replace negative self-talk with positive affirmations. Instead of thinking "I'm not good enough," tell yourself "I am capable, and I am learning."
2. **Visualization:** Imagine yourself succeeding. Picture yourself tackling a challenging task with confidence and ease. This mental exercise can make challenges feel more manageable and less intimidating.
3. **Set Small, Achievable Goals:** Building confidence comes through small wins. Start with easy-to-achieve goals and build up to larger ones. Each success will reinforce your belief in your abilities.
4. **Learn from Failure:** View setbacks as learning opportunities rather than failures. Reframe mistakes as valuable lessons that help you grow.
5. **Seek Feedback:** Sometimes, low confidence stems from not knowing how we're performing. Asking for constructive feedback helps you improve and reinforces that you have room to grow without judgment.
6. **Develop Emotional Resilience:** Practice managing your emotions in high-pressure situations. Meditation, journaling, and mindfulness techniques can help you stay calm and focused.

Alongside the tools above, confidence comes from knowing what you are doing, so if you're preparing for something, becoming competent in that area develops your confidence. Consider any educational exams you may have taken in the past, and how you felt when you had prepared thoroughly for this, did you feel more confident?

What Overcoming Lack of Confidence Will Allow You to Do

When you overcome the barriers of low confidence, you'll unlock new levels of success in all areas of your life. Here's what you can expect:

- **Enhanced Leadership**: You'll be more willing to take charge, lead teams, and make decisions without hesitation.
- **Career Growth**: You'll be more open to pursuing new opportunities and tackling challenges, positioning yourself for promotions and new roles.
- **Improved Relationships**: As your confidence grows, you'll engage more authentically with others, build stronger relationships, and communicate your needs and desires more clearly.

- **Greater Well-Being:** Confidence leads to reduced anxiety, lower stress levels, and increased satisfaction in both your personal and professional life.

By overcoming self-doubt, you'll begin to see yourself as capable of achieving greater things, and this shift will inspire those around you as well.

Conclusion

Confidence is a muscle that grows stronger with practice. The more you invest in strengthening your belief in yourself, the more resilient and capable you become. It's important to recognize that everyone faces moments of self-doubt—what sets successful individuals apart is their ability to push through those moments and move forward regardless. The journey to building confidence is ongoing, but it starts with taking small, intentional steps today.

Call to Action

Now that you've gained insights into the importance of confidence and the tools to build it, it's time to take action. Choose one of the strategies mentioned above and commit to practicing it this week. Set a small goal related to your work or personal life and use that opportunity to build your confidence. Remember, the most powerful way to overcome doubt is through consistent action.

You've got this—start today!

Chapter 2

Growth Mindset vs. Fixed Mindset

Introduction

Dan Carter, the legendary New Zealand All Black, in his fantastic book "The Art of Winning" says "growth mindset is simply the belief that you try to be better tomorrow than you are today, and by doing this on a consistent basis, it leads to becoming a habit"

In the journey toward peak performance, mindset plays a pivotal role. One of the most impactful mindsets you can develop is a *growth mindset*. But what exactly does this mean, and how does it differ from a *fixed mindset*? These two contrasting mindsets shape how we approach challenges, setbacks, and success.

A growth mindset is the belief that abilities and intelligence can be developed over time through effort, learning, and perseverance. In contrast, a fixed mindset is the belief that abilities and intelligence are static, and that our talents are predetermined from birth.

This chapter will delve into the defining characteristics of both mindsets, provide real-life examples of each, and offer tools to help you foster a growth mindset—an essential element for unlocking your potential and achieving lasting success.

Growth and Fixed Mindset in Action

To better understand the difference between a growth and a fixed mindset, let's look at how each plays out in real-life situations.

Growth Mindset in Action

People with a growth mindset view challenges as opportunities for growth. They believe that effort and practice will lead to improvement, and they embrace setbacks as learning experiences.

Example: Sarah is a mid-level manager in a fast-paced tech company. When she faces a difficult project, she doesn't shy away from the challenge. Instead, she embraces it as a chance to learn something new. If her first attempt doesn't succeed, she looks for ways to improve, seeking feedback from colleagues and refining her approach. Sarah's belief

that skills can be developed keeps her motivated and resilient in the face of obstacles.

Key Traits of a Growth Mindset:

- Challenges are opportunities to grow.
- Effort leads to improvement and mastery.
- Failure is viewed as part of the learning process.
- Feedback is valuable for growth.
- Success of others is seen as inspiration.

A colleague once discussed informal learning and provided an example of reading books and listening to podcasts to help growth. This resonated with me, and I put this into action. Following every book, I read and podcast I listened to I captured key take home messages in the notes section of my phone so I could review these later. This process has certainly had a big impact on my growth.

Fixed Mindset in Action

People with a fixed mindset often avoid challenges and may give up easily when things get tough. They believe their abilities are fixed and that effort won't change their natural talent or intelligence. When they fail, they may internalize it as evidence that they are not "good enough."

Example: John is a senior executive who prides himself on being a "natural leader." When he encounters a new task outside of his comfort zone, he feels threatened. After a failed presentation, he assumes he is not cut out for public speaking and avoids it in the future. Rather than seeing this as an area for improvement, he becomes discouraged, and this reluctance to try again holds him back.

Key Traits of a Fixed Mindset:

- Challenges are avoided or feared.
- Effort is seen as pointless or unnecessary.
- Failure is a reflection of inherent limitations.
- Feedback is often ignored or seen as criticism.
- Success of others is viewed as a threat.

Fixed Mindset vs Growth Mindset

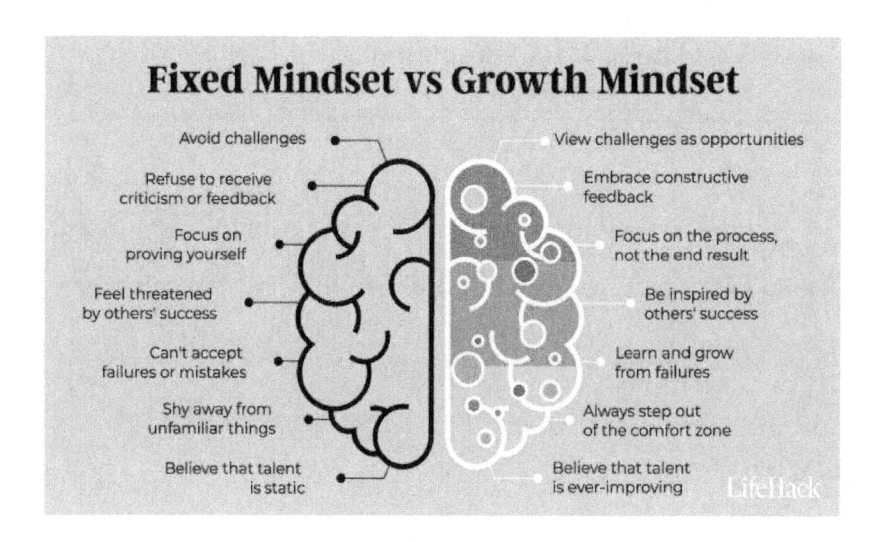

Fixed Mindset:
- Avoid challenges
- Refuse to receive criticism or feedback
- Focus on proving yourself
- Feel threatened by others' success
- Can't accept failures or mistakes
- Shy away from unfamiliar things
- Believe that talent is static

Growth Mindset:
- View challenges as opportunities
- Embrace constructive feedback
- Focus on the process, not the end result
- Be inspired by others' success
- Learn and grow from failures
- Always step out of the comfort zone
- Believe that talent is ever-improving

Interactive Quiz to Measure Your Mindset

Take a moment to reflect on your current mindset. Below is a quick quiz to help you identify whether you lean more toward a growth mindset or a fixed mindset.

For each statement, rate each on a scale of 1 to 5, where 1 = strongly disagree, 2 = disagree,

3 = neutral, 4 = agree and 5 = strongly agree.

- I enjoy taking on new challenges, even if I might fail.
- I believe my abilities can improve with effort and practice.
- When I make a mistake, I focus on what I can learn from it.

- I avoid tasks I think I will fail at.
- I believe other people's success means less success for me.
- I enjoy receiving feedback because it helps me improve.
- I often feel that my abilities are limited and can't be changed.

Scoring:

- Total your points for questions 1, 2, 3, 6 (Growth Mindset).
- Total your points for questions 4, 5, 7 (Fixed Mindset).
- If your growth mindset total is higher, you're on the right track to fostering a growth mindset. If your fixed mindset total is higher, there's room for improvement in shifting your perspective.

Tools to Support a Growth Mindset

Now that you have a better understanding of growth and fixed mindsets, let's explore some tools and strategies that can help you develop a more resilient and expansive mindset.

1. Embrace Challenges

Growth happens outside of your comfort zone. Start by actively seeking challenges, even small ones. Whether it's volunteering for a new project at work or learning a new skill, these challenges will build your confidence and abilities over time.

2. Reframe Failure

Shift your perspective on failure. Rather than seeing failure as a reflection of your capabilities, reframe it as a stepping stone in your development. Each failure offers insights into what works and what doesn't, allowing you to adjust and improve.

3. Focus on Effort, Not Just Outcome

Celebrate the process of learning, not just the results. When you focus on the effort you're putting into growth, rather than just the outcome, you reinforce the belief that effort leads to improvement. This makes the journey more fulfilling and less intimidating.

4. Seek Constructive Feedback

Feedback is one of the most valuable tools for growth. Embrace feedback, both positive and critical, and use it to refine your skills. Constructive feedback helps you identify areas of improvement and fine-tune your approach.

5. Cultivate Self-Compassion

Acknowledge that developing a growth mindset takes time. Be kind to yourself when you fall short. Self-compassion allows you to stay motivated without being overwhelmed by self-criticism.

What Developing a Growth Mindset Will Allow You to Do

Adopting a growth mindset will unlock many opportunities for personal and professional development. Here are some of the powerful outcomes you can expect as you strengthen your growth mindset:

- **Overcome obstacles:** You'll have the resilience to face challenges head-on and find creative solutions when setbacks occur.

- **Enhance learning:** Your ability to adapt and acquire new skills will skyrocket, leading to increased competence and confidence.
- **Boost your resilience:** When faced with adversity, a growth mindset helps you bounce back faster and with greater determination.
- **Increase motivation:** With a growth mindset, you'll find greater satisfaction in the process of improving, leading to long-term motivation.
- **Achieve long-term success:** Since you're focused on growth and effort, success becomes a product of continuous improvement, not a one-time event.

Conclusion

Your mindset shapes your reality. By developing a growth mindset, you open the door to continuous learning, improvement, and success. No longer limited by the belief that your abilities are fixed, you will see challenges as opportunities to evolve, setbacks as lessons, and feedback as a tool for growth.

Call to Action

It's time to take action. Reflect on your current mindset and choose one area of your life where you can implement the tools for cultivating a growth mindset. Start by embracing a challenge, reframing failure, or seeking feedback. Commit to this growth journey today and unlock your full potential. The path to success is yours to create—one step at a time.

Chapter 3
Resilience

What is Resilience?

Resilience is the ability to bounce back from adversity, adapt to challenges, and maintain a sense of control and purpose, even in the face of difficult circumstances. It is not just about surviving hardship; it's about thriving during it. Resilience allows us to navigate setbacks, overcome obstacles, and continue forward with renewed strength and determination.

At its core, resilience is a skill that can be developed and strengthened over time. It's the internal resource that enables you to keep going when things get tough and to see challenges as opportunities for growth rather than insurmountable problems.

Resilience in Action: Hiking to Mont Blanc

A personal example of resilience in action was my journey hiking to Mont Blanc. This experience was not just about hiking the mountain but also about navigating the physical and mental challenges that came with it.

There were moments when the path was treacherous, the weather turned against us, and exhaustion set in, and every step felt heavier. Doubt crept in, and it would have been easy to turn back. But the drive to keep going was fuelled by a deeper purpose—a desire to push my limits, face discomfort, and grow stronger through the experience.

During the climb, resilience meant digging deep, drawing on inner strength, and staying focused on the goal despite the physical pain and mental fatigue. It required an ongoing recalibration of my mindset, shifting my perspective from seeing obstacles as setbacks to viewing them as part of the journey. Each challenge overcome became a reminder of my capability and the power of perseverance.

This adventure taught me that resilience is built in the moments when you choose to keep moving forward, even when the path is uncertain, and the outcome is unknown.

Interactive Quiz to Measure Your Level of Resilience

Take a moment to assess your current level of resilience by answering the following questions. Rate each on a scale of 1 to 5, where 1 = strongly disagree, 2 = disagree,

3 =neutral, 4 = agree and 5 = strongly agree.

Q1. I am able to adapt to changes in my personal or professional life.

Q2. When faced with a challenge, I usually find a way to overcome it.

Q3. I view setbacks as temporary and believe I can learn from them.

Q4. I maintain a positive attitude even when things don't go as planned.

Q5. I believe I can handle whatever comes my way.

Q6. I tend to recover quickly from disappointments or failures.

Q7. I focus on what I can control, rather than what I cannot.

Scoring:

Add up your scores for each question to get a total resilience score.

- **30–35:** High Resilience – You adapt well to challenges and view setbacks as growth opportunities.
- **20–29:** Moderate Resilience – You have a generally positive approach but might benefit from strengthening some resilience skills.
- **7–19:** Low Resilience – You may struggle with adaptability and coping in the face of adversity. Consider exploring resources or coaching to build resilience.

Reflection:

Review your answers. For any statements where you scored a 3 or below, reflect on why these areas might be challenging for you and what steps you might take to develop greater resilience in these areas. This quiz not only provides a score but also invites self-reflection, which can be crucial in building resilience.

Tools to Develop Resilience

Developing resilience is an ongoing process that involves cultivating specific habits and mindsets. Here are some tools to help build resilience:

- **Embrace Challenges:** View challenges as opportunities for growth rather than as threats. When faced with a difficult situation, ask yourself, "What can I learn from this?"
- **Practice Self-Compassion:** Be kind to yourself in moments of failure or difficulty. Self-compassion helps you bounce back by reducing the negative self-talk that can undermine your resilience.
- **Build a Support Network:** Surround yourself with people who encourage and support you. A strong network provides emotional support, guidance, and perspective when you need it most. This was most evident with the team who hiked Mont Blanc together. A group of strangers who came together for 4 days and left being friends for life. Each person during the trip was able to

help another person at different times when they needed that support to keep going. *As Rod Stewart sang in his song "you're in my heart" You're Celtic, United, but baby, I've decided you're the best team I've ever seen, and this team certainly was.*

- **Focus on What You Can Control:** Often, we waste energy on things outside our control. Resilient people focus on their actions, thoughts, and responses, redirecting energy toward things they can influence.
- **Develop a Growth Mindset:** Cultivate a belief that abilities and intelligence can be developed through effort, learning, and persistence. This mindset helps you approach challenges with curiosity and a willingness to improve.
- **Set Clear Goals and Take Action:** Having clear goals gives you direction and purpose, while taking consistent action toward those goals builds confidence and resilience over time.
- **Practice Mindfulness and Reflection:** Regular reflection helps you process experiences, learn from them, and gain insights into your responses. Mindfulness practices like

meditation can enhance emotional regulation and help you stay present, even in stressful situations.

What Having Resilience Will Allow You to Do

Developing resilience transforms how you approach life. It empowers you to:
- **Navigate Uncertainty with Confidence:** Resilience allows you to face the unknown with a sense of calm and determination, knowing that you have the inner resources to adapt and overcome.
- **Overcome Setbacks and Failures:** Instead of being derailed by failure, resilience helps you learn from mistakes and keep moving forward, turning setbacks into stepping stones toward your goals.
- **Maintain Motivation and Purpose:** Even when progress feels slow or challenges seem overwhelming, resilience keeps you connected to your purpose and motivated to keep going.
- **Build Mental Toughness:** Resilience strengthens your mental toughness, enabling you to withstand pressure,

manage stress, and perform at your best, even under challenging conditions.

- **Enhance Emotional Well-being:** By developing resilience, you gain greater control over your emotional responses, reducing anxiety and increasing your overall sense of well-being.

- **Achieve Long-Term Success:** Ultimately, resilience is a key factor in achieving long-term success, both personally and professionally. It equips you with the tools to persevere through adversity, seize opportunities, and reach your full potential.

Conclusion: Resilience as a Lifelong Journey

Resilience is not about avoiding adversity, but about learning to rise every time life knocks us down. Through patience, self-awareness, and the right mindset, we can build the mental and emotional toughness to face challenges head-on. By acknowledging our vulnerabilities and committing to growth, we open the door to a life where setbacks become stepping stones, not roadblocks. Remember, resilience is a journey, not a destination.

The road to success is paved with setbacks so learn to accept they are part of the journey, but with each challenge, you'll grow stronger. The ability to adapt, persevere, and maintain a positive outlook through tough times is within your control.

Call to Action: Building Your Resilience

Take a moment today to reflect on a recent challenge you faced. What did you learn from that experience? How did you grow? Now, write down one small step you can take to strengthen your resilience moving forward. This could be practicing mindfulness, seeking out positive influences, or simply taking time for self-care.

Resilience is like a muscle—it strengthens with consistent use. Make it a point to recognize your progress and continue to invest in your emotional well-being. You're capable of overcoming more than you know. Start today and build the foundation for a resilient future.

Chapter 4
Breaking Free from Overthinking

What is Overthinking?

Overthinking can be described as the habit of dwelling excessively on thoughts and problems, often replaying events in the mind or obsessively

analysing future possibilities.
- In the book enough overthinking by Robert J Charles, he says "overthinking is the critical voice that brings you down because it doubts everybody and everything around you, especially yourself". This mental loop often leads to constant self-questioning and a sense of being stuck. Rather than problem-solving or finding clarity, overthinking magnifies issues and blocks clear decision-making.

Overthinking is like driving around in circles without a destination in sight. Instead of progressing, you end up exhausted, confused, and more anxious than before. While it's natural to reflect on events or ponder future choices, overthinking goes beyond reflection—it becomes a mental trap.

Common forms of overthinking include:
- Rumination: Replaying past mistakes, missed opportunities, or hurtful events.
- Worrying: Projecting negative scenarios or imagining worst-case outcomes in the future.
- Analysis paralysis: Being unable to make decisions because of overanalysing every possible outcome.

The Detrimental Effects of Overthinking on Your Mind and Body

- Overthinking not only clutters your mind but also wreaks havoc on your mental and physical well-being. Here's how:
- Mental Exhaustion: Constantly running through "what ifs" and "should haves" drains mental energy, leaving you fatigued and emotionally depleted. Your brain becomes stuck in a loop, unable to rest or process information effectively.
- Increased Anxiety and Stress: Overthinking triggers the body's stress response, causing elevated cortisol levels. This leads to persistent feelings of anxiety, unease, and sometimes panic.
- Sleep Disruption: Racing thoughts at night prevent relaxation, resulting in insomnia or disrupted sleep patterns. A lack of quality sleep further exacerbates anxiety and contributes to poor mental health.
- Physical Symptoms: The mental strain caused by overthinking can manifest in physical symptoms like headaches, muscle tension, digestive issues, and even weakened immune function.

- Paralysis by Analysis: When you overthink, decision-making becomes impossible. You lose confidence, second-guess yourself, and procrastinate on taking action, which leads to missed opportunities and frustration.

As someone who struggles with overthinking every single day, I know the negative impact this can have on us and our lives.

Interactive Quiz to Measure Your Level of Overthinking

Take a moment to assess your current level of overthinking by answering the following questions. Rate each on a scale of 1 to 5, where 1 = strongly disagree, 2 = disagree, 3=neutral, 4 = agree and 5 = strongly agree.

Q1. When I must make a decision, I often think about it for a long time, going over different possibilities in my head.

Q2. I replay conversations in my mind, wondering if I said the right thing or hw I could have said it differently.

Q3. If I make a mistake, I find myself thinking about it repeatedly, even after it has been resolved

Q4. I frequently worry about things I can't control or that haven't happened yet

Q5. Before starting a new project or task, I tend to go over all the potential outcomes in my head, even if they're unlikely.

Q6. I find it hard to "switch off" my mind when I want to relax or go to sleep because I'm thinking about everything I must do.

Q7. I often imagine worst-case scenarios in everyday situations.

Q8. I feel like I get "stuck" thinking about certain problems or concerns, and it's hard to move on from them.

Q9. I worry about what others think of me or how I appear to others, even in casual interactions.

Q10. I spend a lot of time comparing myself to others or wondering if I measure up.

Scoring:

- **10-20 points:** You tend to be a relaxed thinker. You rarely get bogged down in overthinking.

- **21-30 points**: Moderate overthinking. You sometimes overanalyse but can usually pull yourself out of it.
- **31-40 points**: High overthinking. You may spend a significant amount of time in your head, revisiting the same thoughts or scenarios.
- **41-50 points**: Extreme overthinking. It might be beneficial to explore strategies to help you manage these thought patterns.

Reflection:

If you scored high, consider reflecting on which areas you tend to overthink most and what situations might trigger this. Trying out techniques like mindfulness, journaling, or seeking support can be helpful for breaking overthinking habits.

Tools to Overcome Overthinking

Breaking the habit of overthinking requires intentional strategies to break the cycle of worry and rumination. Here are tools to help:

1. Mindfulness and Grounding Techniques: Mindfulness teaches you to live in the present moment, allowing you to focus on what's happening now rather than getting lost in

past regrets or future worries. Try grounding exercises like deep breathing, body scans, or engaging your five senses to bring your attention back to the here and now.

2. Set Time Limits for Reflection: Allocate a specific amount of time each day (e.g., 15-20 minutes) to think through your concerns or reflect on past events. After this period, intentionally stop and shift focus to something productive or enjoyable.

3. Cognitive Restructuring: Challenge and reframe negative or exaggerated thoughts. Ask yourself:

4. "Is this thought true?"

5. "What's the worst that could happen, and is it realistic?"

6. "What evidence do I have that things might turn out okay?" Restructuring your thought process will help you see situations more rationally.

7. Take Action: Overthinking often comes from indecision. Break tasks into smaller steps and focus on taking one action at a time. By doing something, you reduce the need for endless analysis and create momentum toward your goals.

8. Gratitude Journaling: Writing down three things you are grateful for daily helps shift your focus from what's wrong to what's right. This practice creates a more

positive mindset, reducing the tendency to dwell on negative thoughts.

The Benefits of Breaking Free from Overthinking

- Once you gain control over overthinking, the benefits will extend across every area of your life:
- Mental Clarity and Focus: With less mental clutter, you'll have more space to think clearly, make decisions faster, and focus on what truly matters without second-guessing yourself.
- Reduced Anxiety and Stress: Letting go of excessive thoughts and worries results in a calmer, more relaxed state of mind. You'll feel more in control of your emotions and less prone to stress.
- Improved Sleep and Physical Well-being: A quieter mind leads to better sleep, fewer physical symptoms like headaches and muscle tension, and an overall improvement in your health.
- Increased Productivity: Without the constant loop of indecision, you'll have more energy and time to take

action. Your productivity will increase as you tackle tasks without hesitation or doubt.
- Greater Confidence: Breaking the cycle of overthinking builds self-trust. As you make decisions with clarity and certainty, your confidence will grow, and you'll feel more empowered to pursue your goals.

Conclusion:

Overthinking is a mental habit that takes a toll on your mind, body, and overall quality of life. Recognizing it is the first step toward breaking free. With the right tools—like mindfulness, reframing thoughts, and taking action—you can regain control, reduce anxiety, and live with greater clarity and purpose. The rewards of overcoming overthinking are profound, giving you more confidence, energy, and a deeper sense of well-being.

Now is the time to release yourself from the chains of overthinking and step into a life of clarity, action, and peace.

Call to Action: Take One Step Today

Begin by choosing just one of the tools from this chapter to practice this week. Maybe you decide to label your overthinking cycle or practice a five-minute mindfulness session each morning. Whatever you choose, start small and build on it. Each step you take will strengthen your ability to manage overthinking and move closer to a life of purpose and inner peace.

Chapter 5

Overcoming Imposter Syndrome

Imposter syndrome can feel like a hidden struggle that looms large, often stealing away moments of pride and accomplishment. It's that nagging inner critic, whispering doubts about your achievements, questioning your worth, and diminishing your confidence. For many men in professional fields, imposter syndrome shows up as a quiet, persistent tension, a feeling that no matter how hard you work, you'll eventually be "found out" as undeserving. In this chapter, we'll break down imposter syndrome's impact, explore real-life stories, and provide tools and strategies to recognize and challenge this mindset.

Understanding Imposter Syndrome

Imposter syndrome is the experience of feeling like a fraud or doubting one's abilities, even in the face of tangible achievements and external validation. Originally coined by psychologists Pauline Clance and Suzanne Imes, it affects high achievers who struggle to internalize their success and frequently dismiss their own abilities.

Imposter syndrome isn't simply feeling uncertain—it's a pervasive pattern where self-doubt and a fear of exposure take precedence over self-acknowledgment. As men in executive or demanding roles, you may feel pressure to appear confident and capable, making imposter syndrome a private and often unaddressed experience.

The Impact of Imposter Syndrome

Positive and Negative Examples:

1. Negative Example: Imagine "Daniel," a high-level manager who just delivered a successful project, lauded by his peers and superiors. Despite his success, he feels an underlying sense of inadequacy, believing his achievements are more a matter of luck than skill. This mindset causes Daniel to overwork, constantly striving to "earn" his place, which eventually leads to burnout and strained relationships with his family.
2. Positive Example: Now consider "Adam," who also feels twinges of self-doubt after a promotion. However, Adam

recognizes these feelings as imposter syndrome and begins working on tools to manage them. With practice, he learns to acknowledge his contributions without dismissing them and speaks with a mentor to gain perspective. As a result, Adam's confidence grows, he makes more strategic decisions, and his relationships improve as he gains trust in himself.

These examples show how imposter syndrome, left unchecked, can limit potential, but when acknowledged and managed, it can become a source of growth and resilience.

Imposter syndrome is more common than people may think. In my day job, I work with people who have had very good careers in the professional football game and have lots of knowledge and experience. Especially in the early years of my career, I struggled with imposter syndrome regularly, comparing my knowledge and experiences to them and knowing I never had any career in the professional game. I don't often feel that way now, but It can still be there on occasions.

Here's a self-assessment quiz to help identify how imposter syndrome may be showing up for you. Each type—"Perfectionist," "Expert," and "Soloist"—has unique characteristics, and knowing which resonates with you can provide insights into overcoming imposter syndrome.

Self-Assessment Quiz: What Type of Imposter Syndrome Are You?

For each statement, rate yourself on a scale of 1-5:

1: Rarely True
2: Sometimes True
3: Often True
4: Usually True
5: Always True

Section 1: Perfectionist

3. I feel like I must complete every task flawlessly, and mistakes feel like a failure.
4. I set very high standards for myself and get frustrated when I can't meet them.
5. I find it hard to celebrate my accomplishments because I always see room for improvement.

6. I spend a lot of time refining my work, even when others say it's good enough.
7. *Add up your score for this section. A score of 12 or higher suggests you may lean toward the Perfectionist type.*

Section 2: Expert

8. I feel like I don't know enough to be considered successful, despite my experience or achievements.
9. I constantly seek more certifications, qualifications, or training to feel competent.
10. I avoid taking on tasks unless I'm sure I have all the knowledge or skills needed.
11. I fear that others will realize I lack certain expertise, even though I am considered skilled.
12. *Add up your score for this section. A score of 12 or higher suggests you may lean toward the Expert type.*

Section 3: Soloist

13. I often feel that I must accomplish things on my own and avoid asking for help.
14. When I ask for assistance, I feel like I've failed or that I'm inadequate.

15. I find it hard to delegate tasks because I feel I'm the only one who can do them right.
16. I tend to downplay my success, attributing it to luck or external factors rather than my own abilities.
17. *Add up your score for this section. A score of 12 or higher suggests you may lean toward the Soloist type.*

Quiz Results and Insights:

18. **Perfectionist:** If this was your highest score, you may be experiencing imposter syndrome by constantly feeling your work isn't "good enough." Working on embracing imperfections and setting realistic goals may be key to overcoming these feelings.
19. **Expert:** If you scored highest in this category, you may struggle with feeling "qualified enough." Consider acknowledging the skills you already have and focus on how learning occurs through action rather than perfection.
20. **Soloist:** If Soloist resonated most, you might often feel like you must do things alone. Learning to trust others, delegate, and accept help can alleviate pressure and help you realize your value doesn't hinge on solo efforts.

21. **Reflection:** Use this insight as a guide to approach your imposter syndrome with targeted strategies that align with your type.

Practical Tools

22. **Step-by-Step Approach:** Recognizing and Challenging Negative Thoughts
23. **Awareness:** Start by becoming aware of your inner dialogue. Write down the thoughts that come up when you experience self-doubt.
24. **Identify the Pattern:** Notice recurring themes in your thoughts. Do they centre around perfectionism, fear of failure, or undervaluing your efforts?
25. **Challenge Your Thoughts:** Ask yourself if these thoughts are grounded in reality. Replace negative beliefs with balanced, evidence-based thoughts, focusing on factual accomplishments.
26. **Exercises:**
27. **Daily Wins Journal:** Each day, write down three wins, regardless of their size. This practice builds a record of achievements and reinforces a positive self-image.

28. **Strengths and Skills Inventory:** Create a list of your strengths, skills, and achievements. Revisit it during moments of doubt.
29. **Self-Compassion Practice:** Treat yourself with kindness and understanding. When feelings of inadequacy arise, ask, "What would I say to a friend feeling this way?"
30. **Digital Recommendations:**
31. **Mindfulness Apps (e.g., Calm, Headspace):** Building mindfulness helps manage self-doubt and brings awareness to automatic thought patterns.
32. **Thought Diary Apps (e.g., Thought Diary, Reflect):** Journaling apps can guide structured reflections and track your progress over time.

Interactive Questions

- To make this journey engaging and reflective, try these interactive elements:
- Buddy Check-In: Find a trusted colleague or friend to exchange experiences with, keeping each other accountable to acknowledge strengths and minimize self-doubt.
- Reflection Prompts: Use prompts like "How did I contribute to my achievements today?" or "What skills

did I rely on to reach my goals?" Set these prompts as reminders to appear in your calendar weekly.\

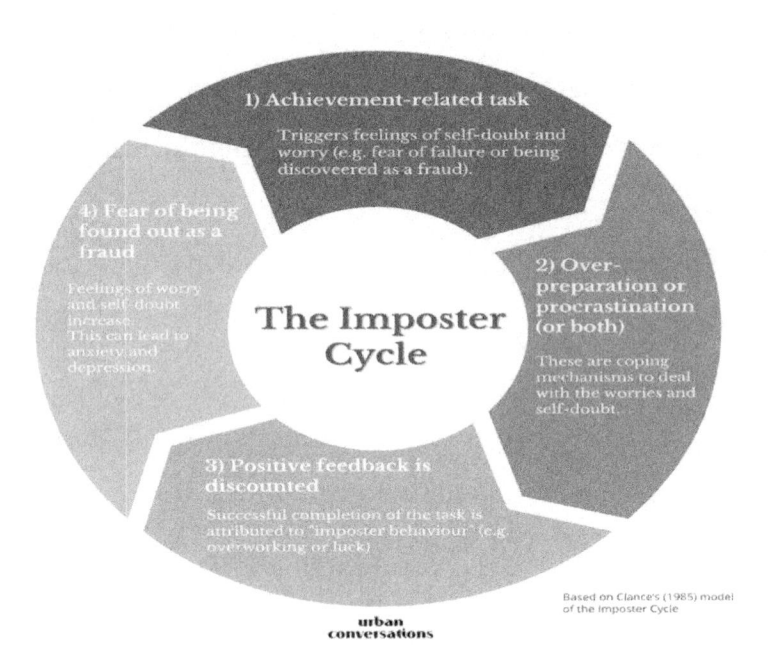

The Imposter Cycle

1) Achievement-related task
Triggers feelings of self-doubt and worry (e.g. fear of failure or being discovered as a fraud).

2) Over-preparation or procrastination (or both)
These are coping mechanisms to deal with the worries and self-doubt.

3) Positive feedback is discounted
Successful completion of the task is attributed to "imposter behaviour" (e.g. overworking or luck).

4) Fear of being found out as a fraud
Feelings of worry and self-doubt increase. This can lead to anxiety and depression.

Based on Clance's (1985) model of the Imposter Cycle

urban conversations

What Overcoming Imposter Syndrome Will Allow You to Do

Freeing yourself from imposter syndrome can unlock a clearer perspective on your value and abilities. It can foster a mindset where taking risks feels less daunting, and self-trust becomes a guiding principle in your decisions. As you develop this confidence, you'll notice an enhanced sense of calm in your role, allowing you to lead with authenticity and resilience. Letting go of imposter syndrome means having the freedom to step into opportunities, build stronger relationships, and focus on growth rather than constantly needing external validation.

Call to Action: Embrace Your Journey

Overcoming imposter syndrome isn't about eliminating all doubt but recognizing its impact and learning to manage it. Challenge yourself this week: Acknowledge one of your recent accomplishments fully. Sit with the feeling and try not to diminish it with self-doubt. Set one intentional goal that highlights your strengths.

Through this journey, let imposter syndrome become a reminder of how far you've come rather than an obstacle. Embrace each step as part of your growth, knowing that you're not alone, and that each small victory builds the foundation of a resilient, self-assured minds

Chapter 6
Breaking the Chains of Procrastination

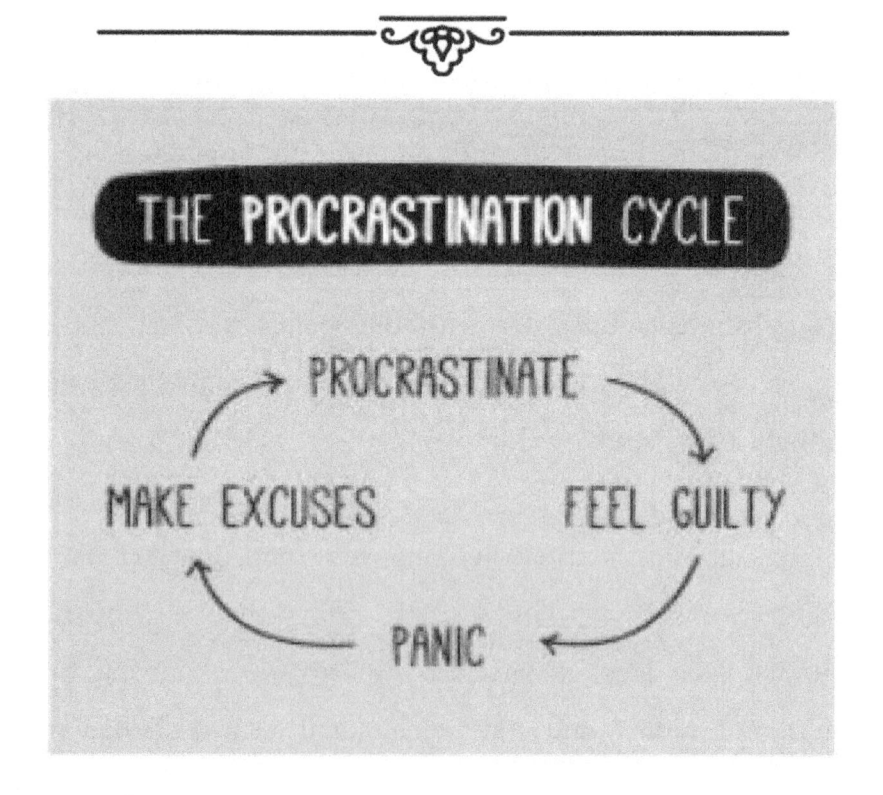

THE PROCRASTINATION CYCLE

PROCRASTINATE → FEEL GUILTY → PANIC → MAKE EXCUSES → (repeat)

Introduction

Procrastination is an invisible barrier that subtly yet persistently holds us back from reaching our fullest potential. Despite knowing the benefits of taking action, we often find ourselves delaying important tasks, convincing ourselves that we'll get to them "later." This chapter aims to explore procrastination from every angle, helping you understand why you procrastinate, how it impacts your life, and, most importantly, the tools to overcome it. Remember, tackling procrastination isn't about forcing yourself to work harder—it's about changing how you think and approach the tasks in front of you. In a google search, in one study 84% of the population say they have procrastinated at one point or another.

Procrastination in Action

Have you ever put off a deadline, then spent the entire week stressed about the task, only to start working on it at the last minute? Or maybe you've scrolled through social media instead of doing something meaningful, only to feel guilty afterward. This is procrastination in action: it's not simply avoiding work, but rather a series of mental games we play with ourselves, rooted in fear, self-doubt, and sometimes even perfectionism. We procrastinate when tasks feel overwhelming or when we fear failure. In this section, we'll look at various forms of procrastination and the excuses we tell ourselves, helping you recognize it in your own life.

Interactive Quiz to Measure Your Level of Procrastination

Take a moment to assess your current level of Procrastination by answering the following questions. Rate each on a scale of 1 to 5, where 1 = strongly disagree, 2 = disagree, 3=neutral, 4 = agree and 5 = strongly agree.

1. I find myself putting off tasks even when I know they are important.
2. I wait until the last minute to start tasks.
3. I often feel anxious or guilty when I'm not doing what I know I should be.
4. I tend to prioritize short-term enjoyment over long-term goals.
5. I frequently avoid tasks that feel challenging or unfamiliar.
6. I struggle to stick to plans or deadlines.
7.

Score Interpretation:

- **6–12**: Minimal procrastinator – You generally stay on top of things, though minor tweaks can help.
- **13–20**: Moderate procrastinator – You may delay certain tasks, especially if they're difficult or unappealing.

- **21–30**: Frequent procrastinator – Procrastination significantly impacts your productivity. Learning new strategies could be transformative.

Tools to Overcome Procrastination

1. **Time Chunking** – Divide tasks into manageable chunks and assign specific times for each. Known as the Pomodoro Technique, setting a timer for focused work (25 minutes) followed by a 5-minute break can help prevent burnout and increase focus.
2. **Set Micro-Goals** – Large tasks are often overwhelming. Break them down into smaller, achievable goals that allow you to make consistent progress and feel a sense of accomplishment.
3. **Prioritization with the Eisenhower Matrix** – Classify tasks into four categories: Important/Urgent, Important/Not Urgent, Not Important/Urgent, and Not Important/Not Urgent. Prioritize based on importance and urgency to prevent busywork from overtaking meaningful tasks.
4. **Address the Root Cause** – Many people procrastinate because of deeper issues like fear of failure, perfectionism, or lack of confidence. Take a moment to ask yourself why

you're avoiding a task, then address the underlying concern with a specific action.

5. **Accountability Partner** – Share your goals with someone who will help keep you on track. This could be a friend, colleague, or a coach. Knowing that someone else is rooting for your success can provide a powerful boost.

6. **Visualization Techniques** – Picture the benefits of completing the task versus the costs of delaying it. Visualization strengthens your motivation and helps reduce procrastination.

What Overcoming Procrastination Will Allow You to Do

Imagine the mental clarity, confidence, and fulfilment that come from consistently acting on your intentions. Overcoming procrastination doesn't just make you more productive—it allows you to feel in control of your life, improves your relationships, and enhances your self-esteem. When you stop putting off the things that matter, you open up a world of possibilities. Your energy shifts from guilt and stress to excitement and empowerment, allowing you to pursue new goals and dreams without hesitation.

Conclusion

Procrastination can feel like a life sentence, keeping us trapped in cycles of delay, frustration, and self-doubt. However, as you've seen, it is a habit we can break with awareness, strategy, and the right tools. Whether it's setting micro-goals, chunking your time, or finding an accountability partner, remember that small changes can lead to substantial results. The key is to be patient with yourself and committed to progress, no matter how gradual.

Call to Action

Take the first step today. Choose one task you've been putting off and use one of the tools above to tackle it. Feel the satisfaction of moving forward, even if it's just a small step. Reflect on how good it feels to be in control, and remember: overcoming procrastination is a journey, but every action you take today brings you one step closer to your goals.

Chapter 7

Overcoming Anxiety

Introduction

Anxiety has a way of creeping into our lives in different shapes and forms, often when we least expect it. For many men in high-performance roles, anxiety can emerge as a background hum—sometimes too subtle to notice, other times too powerful to ignore. It can disrupt focus, increase self-doubt, and drain energy, making even small decisions feel like significant hurdles. Whether you're facing big career challenges, struggling to maintain balance in your personal life, or simply feeling the weight of expectations, anxiety is a universal response to stress.

In this chapter, we'll dig into what anxiety is, explore the ways it manifests in our lives, and provide tools to help you not just manage but also reduce it. By the end, you'll see how overcoming anxiety can be a transformative step toward achieving your peak potential.

Anxiety in Action

Anxiety can manifest in various ways, and it often differs from person to person. For some, it's a constant sense of dread or an undefined worry lingering in the background. For others, anxiety strikes suddenly in specific situations, like before a major presentation or during high-stakes decision-making. Here are a few common ways anxiety can show up in our professional and personal lives:

1. **Indecision:** You may find yourself overthinking simple choices, delaying decisions, or second-guessing yourself repeatedly.
2. **Perfectionism and Procrastination:** Anxiety can push you toward perfectionism, where you put off tasks until everything feels "just right," leading to procrastination.
3. **Physical Symptoms:** Sometimes, anxiety manifests physically through tension headaches, shallow breathing, a tight chest, or even stomach issues.
4. **Impulsivity:** Under stress, some people react quickly and impulsively, as a way to break free from anxious thoughts. This can lead to hasty decisions that may not align with long-term goals.

Anxiety can feel all-encompassing, but it's essential to remember that it is manageable. Recognizing these patterns is the first step to transforming your response to anxiety, putting you back in control.

Interactive Quiz: Measure Your Level of Anxiety

Let's assess where you currently stand in terms of anxiety. This quiz is designed to help you gauge your anxiety levels by answering a few questions honestly. Rate yourself on a scale of 1 to 5, with 1 = Never, 2 = Rarely, 3 = Sometimes, 4 = Often and 5 = Always.

- I find myself unable to stop worrying about work, even when I'm off the clock.
- I have trouble focusing on tasks because of anxious thoughts.
- I often feel overwhelmed by my responsibilities.
- I avoid certain tasks or situations out of fear.
- My sleep is frequently disturbed by worry or stress.
- Once you've answered, add up your score:
- **5-10**: Low anxiety – You experience anxiety occasionally, but it likely doesn't disrupt your life significantly.
- **11-15**: Moderate anxiety – Anxiety may impact certain aspects of your life, but you generally maintain control.

- **16-20**: High anxiety – Anxiety often disrupts your routine, impacting both work and personal life.
- **21-25**: Severe anxiety – Your anxiety may feel overwhelming and require more focused strategies to manage effectively.

Keep this score in mind as we go through some tools to help you manage your anxiety.

Tools to Overcome Anxiety

Here are some proven tools and techniques to help you reduce anxiety and regain control:

1. **Mindful Breathing**: When anxiety strikes, start by slowing down your breathing. Breathe in deeply through your nose, hold for a few seconds, and exhale slowly through your mouth. This helps ground you in the present moment and reduces physical symptoms.
2. **Identify Thought Patterns**: Keep track of recurring anxious thoughts in a journal. Are there specific triggers? Do you tend to focus on worst-case scenarios? Challenging these thought patterns can help break the anxiety loop.

3. **Physical Activity:** Exercise can significantly reduce anxiety by releasing endorphins and clearing your mind. Even a 10-minute walk can make a noticeable difference.
4. **Set Boundaries and Limits:** If work or personal obligations are overwhelming you, take a step back to evaluate where you can set boundaries. Saying no to non-essential commitments can create more room for self-care and lower anxiety.
5. **Visualization Techniques:** Imagine yourself facing a stressful situation with confidence. Picture yourself staying calm, clear-headed, and making good decisions. Visualization can help shift your mindset from anxiety to capability.
6. **Gradual Exposure:** If certain situations trigger anxiety, consider facing them in small, manageable steps. For example, if public speaking causes stress, practice giving short, low-stakes presentations to build confidence over time.
7. **Professional Support:** If your anxiety feels unmanageable, seeking guidance from a coach or therapist can provide personalized support to help you regain control and find effective coping mechanisms.

What Overcoming Anxiety Will Allow You to Do

Overcoming anxiety is about reclaiming your energy, focus, and peace of mind. Here's what that could look like in action:

- **Improved Decision-Making**: You'll be able to make clearer, more confident decisions without being bogged down by self-doubt.
- **Enhanced Productivity**: As you free up mental space previously occupied by anxiety, you'll be more effective and focused, enabling you to accomplish tasks more efficiently.
- **Stronger Relationships**: When you're not preoccupied with anxious thoughts, you'll find it easier to connect meaningfully with colleagues, friends, and family.
- **Increased Resilience**: Overcoming anxiety doesn't mean you'll never feel it again. Instead, you'll have the tools to handle it when it arises, making you more resilient in the face of new challenges.

Overcoming anxiety isn't about eliminating all worries but about learning to navigate them. By practicing these strategies, you can transform how you respond to stress and open up new possibilities for growth.

Conclusion

Anxiety is a common experience, especially for men in high-performance roles, but it doesn't have to control your life. Through awareness, the right tools, and a commitment to personal growth, you can reduce anxiety's impact and build a life where it no longer holds you back. Remember, overcoming anxiety doesn't happen overnight. It's a journey, one you're fully capable of walking with confidence.

Call to Action

Now that you've completed this chapter, take a moment to review your anxiety score and consider setting a small, achievable goal for yourself. This could be practicing mindful breathing daily, journaling your thoughts, or scheduling a meeting with a coach to discuss your journey. Commit to making one change this week to start reducing anxiety's hold on your life. As you take each step, you'll find yourself moving closer to a stronger, more confident version of yourself—one that's ready to achieve your peak potential.

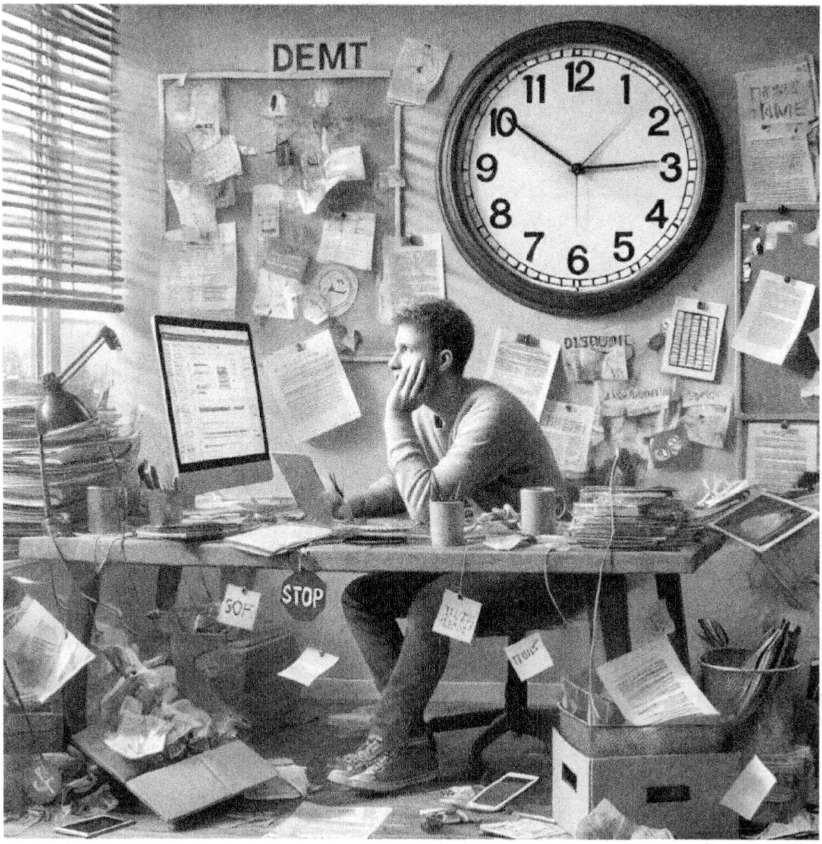
DEMT
STOP

Chapter 8
Overcoming Self-Sabotage

Introduction

Self-sabotage is an invisible force that holds many people back from achieving their full potential. It's the silent struggle behind procrastination, perfectionism, and the tendency to put off the very actions that could move us forward. Often, we aren't even aware we're doing it, making it one of the most insidious obstacles to personal and professional growth. This chapter is dedicated to helping you understand, recognize, and conquer self-sabotage. It's time to shed light on the habits, beliefs, and mental barriers holding you back so you can finally unlock the doors to your true potential.

Self-Sabotage in Action

Self-sabotage manifests in various forms, often disguised as behaviours or thought patterns we consider "normal" or "acceptable." Here are a few common ways it shows up:

1. **Procrastination** – Delaying actions, projects, or decisions until the last moment, creating stress and diminishing the quality of your work.
2. **Perfectionism** – Believing that if something isn't perfect, it's not worth doing. This can prevent you from taking risks, trying new things, or putting your work out into the world.
3. **Negative Self-Talk** – Criticizing yourself constantly, doubting your abilities, or fixating on your flaws can erode self-esteem and create a cycle of failure.
4. **Fear of Success** – As strange as it sounds, the fear of success can lead to self-sabotage. Some people worry that achieving their goals might change their lives in ways they can't control.
5. **Over-Commitment** – Taking on too much can lead to burnout, making it impossible to focus on what really matters. This prevents meaningful progress.

Recognizing self-sabotage in action is the first step to overcoming it. By learning to identify these patterns, you can begin to take back control of your actions and your life.

Interactive Quiz: Measure Your Level of Self-Sabotage

Use this quick quiz to gauge how much self-sabotage is affecting your life. Rate yourself on a scale of 1 to 5, with 1 = Never, 2 = Rarely, 3 = Sometimes, 4 = Often and 5 = Always.

- I find myself putting off important tasks until the last minute.
- I avoid setting ambitious goals because I doubt my ability to achieve them.
- I feel like if my work isn't perfect, I've failed.
- I often let self-doubt stop me from sharing my ideas or work.
- I regularly criticize myself, even for minor mistakes.
- I take on too many commitments and then struggle to complete them all.
- I feel afraid of what achieving my goals might mean for my relationships, career, or life.
- I notice myself avoiding feedback or constructive criticism, fearing it will reinforce my doubts.

Scoring:

- **8–16:** Minimal self-sabotage. You're on a solid path!

- **17–24**: Moderate self-sabotage. Some behaviours may be holding you back from your full potential.
- **25–32**: High self-sabotage. Self-limiting habits and beliefs are likely affecting your personal and professional life.
- **33–40**: Extreme self-sabotage. You're likely engaging in regular patterns that hinder growth and fulfilment. It may be helpful to seek additional guidance.

Tools to Overcome Self-Sabotage

1. **Self-Awareness Practices**

    Regular self-reflection through journaling or meditation can help you identify when self-sabotaging behaviours creep in. Writing down your thoughts and reactions can reveal patterns, allowing you to catch yourself in the act and make different choices.

2. **Set Manageable Goals**

    Break down large, daunting goals into smaller, achievable steps. Instead of focusing on the end result, direct your energy towards manageable actions that build momentum and confidence over time.

3. **Challenge Negative Self-Talk**

    Recognize when your inner critic speaks up and learn to counter it with positive affirmations. Remind yourself of your strengths and previous achievements. Replace "I can't" with "I can try" and "I failed" with "I learned."

4. **Practice Self-Compassion**

   Treat yourself with kindness, especially after setbacks. Perfectionism often stems from an inability to forgive our own mistakes. Remember, every failure is a stepping stone toward growth.

5. **Visualize Success and Embrace Your Potential**

   Instead of fearing what success might bring, visualize your future self-thriving. Picture the benefits of achieving your goals – increased confidence, financial security, or fulfilling relationships – and allow these positive images to motivate you.

What Overcoming Self-Sabotage Will Allow You to Do

When you overcome self-sabotage, your potential becomes limitless. Without these internal barriers, you'll be able to take risks, pursue new opportunities, and feel a sense of pride and purpose in your achievements. You'll notice your confidence growing, as self-doubt no longer dominates your thoughts. By no longer holding yourself back, you will start to see more opportunities, create better relationships, and achieve goals that previously seemed out of reach. Most importantly, you'll gain the freedom to be authentically yourself, embracing and nurturing your unique strengths.

Conclusion

Self-sabotage is something that everyone faces, but it doesn't have to be a permanent part of your life. By understanding the triggers and habits that lead to self-sabotage, you've already taken the first step toward breaking the cycle. This journey requires patience, self-compassion, and commitment, but the rewards are immeasurable. You have the power to become your own biggest ally and accomplish goals you never thought possible.

Call to Action

As you reflect on this chapter, think about one area of your life where you see self-sabotage showing up. Is it in your career, relationships, or personal goals? Take a moment to write down a specific action you can take to combat this pattern. Share it with someone you trust or keep it as a commitment to yourself. Remember, the journey to overcoming self-sabotage starts with a single step. Embrace the change, trust in your potential, and begin moving forward today.

Chapter 9
Overcoming Dopamine Addiction

Introduction

In the modern world, we are constantly surrounded by stimuli that trigger our brain's reward system, making it harder than ever to maintain focus, discipline, and emotional well-being. This system relies heavily on a neurotransmitter called dopamine, often referred to as the "feel-good" chemical. While dopamine is essential for motivation, pleasure, and learning, too much of it can lead to unhealthy habits that keep us stuck in cycles of instant gratification. Over time, we can become addicted to this constant dopamine rush, leading to negative consequences for our mental and physical health.

This chapter will explore the phenomenon of dopamine addiction, how it manifests in our everyday lives, particularly through social media and poor eating habits, and provide you with practical tools to break free from this cycle.

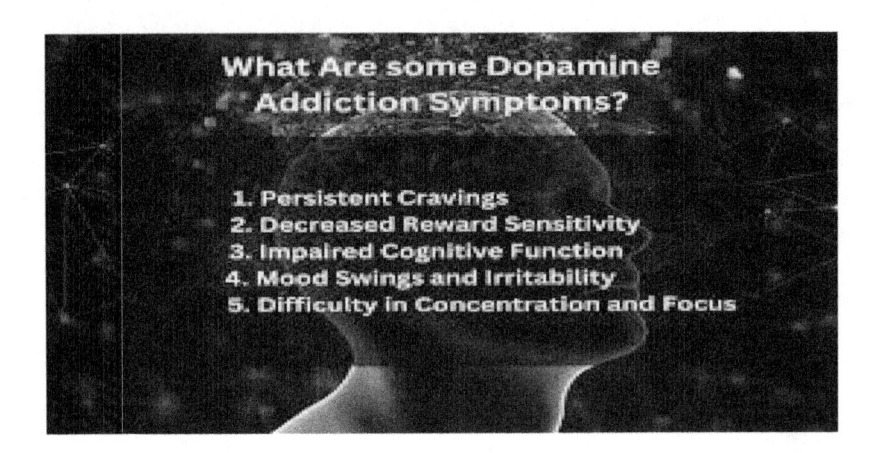

What Are some Dopamine Addiction Symptoms?

1. Persistent Cravings
2. Decreased Reward Sensitivity
3. Impaired Cognitive Function
4. Mood Swings and Irritability
5. Difficulty in Concentration and Focus

Dopamine Addiction in Action

Dopamine addiction isn't about drug abuse or alcohol dependency—though those can certainly be factors. It's more subtle, affecting the choices we make on a daily basis. From mindlessly scrolling through social media to consuming unhealthy foods, our behaviour is often driven by the need to experience that next dopamine hit.

Social Media and Dopamine

Social media is perhaps one of the most insidious forms of dopamine addiction. Every notification, like, comment, or share sends a signal to the brain that reinforces the behaviour. This cycle of intermittent reinforcement, where rewards come unpredictably, is incredibly powerful. The more time you spend on social media, the more your brain starts to crave that instant gratification. Over time, you may find it harder to focus on longer-term goals or more meaningful interactions, as your brain becomes accustomed to the fleeting rewards of online engagement.

Poor Eating Habits and Dopamine

Another common area where dopamine addiction plays out is in our relationship with food. Sugary, fatty, and processed foods trigger a release of dopamine, which is why many people turn to these foods for comfort or emotional regulation. The pleasure derived from eating such foods can create a cycle of cravings, where you seek out that "feel-good" moment, often at the expense of your health. Just like with social media, the more you give in to these cravings, the more your brain craves them.

Interactive Quiz: Measure Your Level of Dopamine Addiction

Take a moment to reflect on your own habits by answering the following questions. Rate yourself on a scale of 1 to 5, with 1 = Never, 2 = Rarely, 3 = Sometimes, 4 = Often and 5 = Always.

1. I find myself scrolling through social media apps more often than I intend to.
2. I often seek out sugary or comfort foods when I'm stressed or anxious.
3. I struggle to focus on tasks that don't provide immediate rewards or satisfaction.
4. I feel restless or irritable when I don't receive notifications on my phone.
5. I frequently choose short-term pleasures (e.g., snacks, social media) over long-term goals (e.g., work, fitness).
6. I often procrastinate on important tasks in favour of easier, more rewarding activities.

Scoring:

- 6-10: Low risk of dopamine addiction. You may have healthy habits but still indulge in occasional pleasures.
- 11-15: Moderate risk of dopamine addiction. You may need to re-evaluate your habits to ensure they're not affecting your well-being.
- 16-20: High risk of dopamine addiction. Your habits may be significantly impacting your mental and physical health, and it's time to take proactive steps to regain control.

Tools to Overcome Dopamine Addiction

Breaking free from dopamine addiction requires intentionality and the use of practical tools. Here are some strategies that can help you regain control:

1. Digital Detox

1. Start by scheduling time away from screens. Try a "phone-free" hour each day or designate one day a week to be free of social media. Use this time for more meaningful activities such as reading, exercising, or spending time with loved ones. Over time, you will begin to rewire your brain to seek fulfilment from sources other than digital rewards.

2. **2. Mindful Eating**
3. When it comes to food, practice mindful eating. Pay attention to what you're eating, how it makes you feel, and why you're eating it. Are you truly hungry, or are you seeking a dopamine fix? By becoming more aware of your eating habits, you can reduce the tendency to reach for unhealthy foods out of habit or emotional triggers.
4. **3. Set Long-Term Goals**
5. To counteract the short-term rewards from dopamine-triggering activities, set long-term goals that provide deeper, more lasting satisfaction. Whether it's personal growth, fitness, or career development, focus on the progress you're making toward meaningful goals, even when the rewards aren't immediate.
6. **4. Practice Gratitude**
7. Gratitude practices can help rewire your brain to focus on the positive aspects of your life, without needing constant external validation. Take a few minutes each day to reflect on what you're grateful for. This can help shift your focus from instant gratification to long-term fulfilment.
8. **5. Build Healthy Habits**

9. Replace dopamine-triggering behaviours with healthier alternatives. For example, instead of scrolling through social media when you're bored, go for a walk, read, or practice a hobby. Over time, these new habits will provide you with more sustainable forms of satisfaction and fulfilment.

What Overcoming Dopamine Addiction Will Allow You to Do

By taking control of your dopamine-driven behaviours, you'll free up energy and focus for the things that truly matter. Here are some benefits you'll experience:

- **Increased Focus and Productivity**: Without constant distractions, you'll be able to concentrate on important tasks and projects that align with your long-term goals.
- **Improved Emotional Resilience**: You'll learn to cope with stress, anxiety, and boredom without relying on external sources of comfort.
- **Enhanced Relationships**: By stepping away from social media, you'll have more time and mental space to connect with loved ones in a meaningful way.

- **Better Health:** Healthier eating habits and less reliance on quick dopamine fixes will improve your physical and mental well-being.
- **A Greater Sense of Fulfilment:** You'll find more joy in pursuing long-term goals and personal growth, rather than seeking fleeting rewards.

Conclusion

Dopamine addiction is a powerful force in today's world, shaping many of our daily decisions and behaviours. However, by understanding its impact and taking intentional steps to reduce our reliance on quick rewards, we can reclaim control over our lives. Overcoming dopamine addiction is a process, but the rewards—improved focus, health, and emotional well-being—are well worth the effort.

Call to Action

If you found this chapter helpful, it's time to take action. Start by using the tools provided and commit to taking one small step each day to break free from dopamine addiction. Whether it's setting boundaries for social media use, practicing mindful eating, or focusing on long-term goals, every action you take will bring you closer to a more balanced and fulfilling life.

Don't wait for the perfect moment—start today and take control of your dopamine-driven behaviours now!

Chapter 10
Overcoming Fear

Introduction

Fear is one of the most common and powerful emotions we experience. It's deeply rooted in our survival instincts, designed to protect us from danger. However, in today's world, fear often arises in situations that are not life-threatening but can feel just as intense. It can manifest as self-doubt, anxiety, or even physical symptoms like a racing heart or sweaty palms. This chapter is dedicated to understanding fear, identifying its impact on your life, and learning how to overcome it so that you can unlock your true potential.

Fear in Action

Fear can take many forms. It might show up as the voice in your head telling you that you're not good enough to tackle a new challenge, or the paralyzing sensation you get when thinking about taking a step outside your comfort zone. It's the impulse that keeps you from making bold decisions or pursuing your dreams, often resulting in procrastination, missed opportunities, and a life led by hesitation.

The thing about fear is that it is often based on false assumptions. It feeds off uncertainty, but the reality is that many of the things we fear are not as dangerous as we imagine. For example, the fear of public speaking or failure may stop you from presenting ideas or going after that promotion, yet the truth is that taking action in these situations usually leads to growth, learning, and unexpected rewards. Fear works by keeping us in a state of inertia, but action is the antidote to fear.

Interactive Quiz to Measure Your Level of Fear

Take a few moments to reflect on your current experience with fear. Use this simple quiz to measure your level of fear and identify areas where it may be holding you back.

Instructions: Rate yourself on a scale of 1 to 5, with 1 = Never, 2 = Rarely, 3 = Sometimes, 4 = Often and 5 = Always.

1. I often feel overwhelmed by the thought of failure.

2. I avoid situations where I might make a mistake.
3. I fear judgment from others when I express my opinions or ideas.
4. I hold back from pursuing opportunities because I feel unsure of my abilities.
5. I often overthink potential negative outcomes before taking action.
6. I experience physical symptoms (e.g., sweaty palms, racing heart) when faced with a challenge.
7. I let fear dictate my choices, even when I know better.

Scoring:

- **7–14 points:** Fear may not be a major obstacle for you right now, but it's still worth acknowledging when it arises.
- **15–24 points:** You are moderately affected by fear, and it may be holding you back from reaching your full potential.
- **25–35 points:** Fear is likely a significant barrier in your life, influencing many of your decisions and actions. It's time to face it head-on.

Tools to Overcome Fear

Overcoming fear is not about eliminating it entirely; it's about learning how to move forward despite it. Here are some powerful tools to help you manage and overcome fear:

1. **Reframe Your Thoughts:** Fear often thrives on negative thinking. Challenge your fearful thoughts by asking, "What's the worst that can happen?" Often, the worst is not as bad as it seems, and taking a positive action can change your perspective.

2. **Breathing Techniques:** Deep breathing can help calm your nervous system when fear takes over. Try the 4-7-8 breathing technique: inhale for 4 counts, hold for 7 counts, and exhale for 8 counts. Repeat this several times to reduce the physiological effects of fear.

3. **Visualization:** Imagine yourself successfully navigating a fearful situation. Visualize the positive outcomes, your calm demeanour, and the satisfaction of overcoming the fear. This exercise can help reprogram your subconscious mind.

4. **Gradual Exposure:** Fear often lessens the more we face it. Start small. If you're afraid of public speaking, begin by speaking in front of a mirror, then to a small group of

friends, and gradually work your way up. Exposure helps desensitize your fear over time.

5. **Affirmations:** Use positive affirmations to counteract negative self-talk. Repeat statements like, "I am capable," "I trust myself," and "I am confident in my abilities." These affirmations help shift your mindset towards action.

6. **Focus on What You Can Control:** Fear thrives on uncertainty. Focus on the elements you can control, and take deliberate, small actions towards your goals. This builds confidence and reduces fear's grip.

What Overcoming Fear Will Allow You to Do

When you overcome fear, you unlock a world of possibilities. Fear often acts as a barrier between where you are now and where you want to be. By facing your fears, you can:

- **Take Bold Action:** Fear often keeps us stuck in comfort zones, but overcoming it allows you to make decisions with confidence, pursue opportunities, and take risks that lead to personal and professional growth.

- **Build Resilience:** Each time you face your fears, you become stronger and more resilient. You'll develop the

mental toughness to handle challenges with grace and agility.
- **Achieve Your Potential:** Fear can cloud your judgment and limit your actions. By confronting it, you can tap into your true potential, pursue your passions, and create the life you desire.
- **Inspire Others:** When you lead by example and show others that fear doesn't have to control your life, you inspire them to do the same. This creates a ripple effect, spreading confidence and courage in your community.

Conclusion

Fear is a natural emotion, but it doesn't have to dictate your life. By understanding fear, using tools to overcome it, and consistently taking action, you can break free from its grip. Fear loses its power when you confront it, and in doing so, you gain control over your future.

Call to Action

Now that you have the tools and insights to overcome fear, take the first step. Identify one fear that is currently holding you back—whether it's a fear of failure, rejection, or the unknown—and commit to taking one action towards overcoming it today. Share your journey with someone you trust and hold yourself accountable for your progress. Remember, the only way to defeat fear is to face it head-on.

Start small but start now. Your future self will thank you.

Chapter 11

Breaking Free from Validation

Introduction

Easy to become dependent on validation. Whether it's In a world driven by likes, comments, and external approval, praiseit's at work, attention from peers, or the recognition of accomplishments, seeking validation can sometimes become the lens through which we view our self-worth. But here's the truth: while external validation can feel rewarding in the short term, it's a hollow foundation for personal growth and lasting confidence. True empowerment comes from within, and breaking free from the need for constant external approval can unlock a whole new level of personal freedom, self-esteem, and achievement.

This chapter will help you understand why we seek validation, how it impacts our mindset and behaviour, and provide practical tools to break free from this cycle. By the end, you will be equipped to build your internal sense of validation and step into your true potential.

Seeking Validation in Action

Validation-seeking can manifest in many ways, often subtly shaping our decisions and reactions. Some common examples include:

- **Constant Comparison:** Looking at what others are doing, often feeling inferior or questioning your own path based on others' success.
- **Perfectionism:** The belief that only perfect outcomes will earn you praise, leading to procrastination or burnout.
- **People-Pleasing:** The need to say yes to others, even when it conflicts with your own needs, just to gain approval.
- **Fear of Rejection:** Holding back from making bold decisions or taking risks because of the potential judgment or criticism from others.

These patterns of behaviour limit your growth and self-expression because they are driven by an external need to be seen or approved. When we rely on the validation of others, we place our power in their hands, leaving us vulnerable and unable to fully step into our authentic selves.

Interactive Quiz: Measure Your Level of Needing Validation

Take a moment to reflect on your current level of seeking validation. Rate yourself on a scale of 1 to 5, with 1 = Never, 2 = Rarely, 3 = Sometimes, 4 = Often and 5 = Always.

1. I often compare myself to others to gauge my success or worth.
2. I feel anxious when I haven't received feedback or recognition for my work.
3. I sometimes make decisions based on what others might think, rather than what feels right to me.
4. I seek praise or compliments to feel good about myself.
5. I avoid taking risks if I think it might lead to criticism.
6. I often feel unsure about my accomplishments until others acknowledge them.

Scoring:

- 6-12: You may have a low need for validation and are likely comfortable with your own self-worth.
- 13-20: You seek validation occasionally, but it doesn't define your confidence or decision-making.

- 21-30: You may have a moderate need for external validation that could be limiting your full potential.
- 31-36: You may be highly reliant on validation, which could be affecting your self-esteem and growth.

If your score is on the higher end, this chapter will be especially beneficial for you as you work on freeing yourself from this external dependence.

Tools to Overcome Needing Validation

Now that you understand how validation-seeking shows up in your life, let's explore some powerful tools to break free from this pattern.

1. **Self-Awareness and Reflection:**
   Take time to reflect on your core values and what truly matters to you. When you know what you stand for, external opinions become less significant. Journaling or meditation can help you gain clarity on what drives you beyond the approval of others.
2. **Practice Self-Compassion:**
   We can be our own worst critics, often demanding perfection from ourselves. Replace self-criticism with self-compassion. Treat yourself the way you would treat a close friend—with kindness and understanding. This

practice helps you detach from the need for external praise.

3. **Shift Your Focus to Process, Not Outcome:**
When you focus too much on the end result or recognition, you miss the joy of the journey. Shift your mindset to focus on the process and personal growth, not just on external outcomes. Celebrate small wins that reinforce your effort, not just achievements.

4. **Set Internal Goals:**
Instead of waiting for external recognition, set goals that are internally driven. These might be about personal growth, learning, or mastery in a skill. Internal goals shift the focus from external validation to personal fulfilment and achievement.

5. **Surround Yourself with Supportive People:**
Seek relationships with people who uplift you for who you are, not just for what you do. A supportive network can help reinforce your sense of worth without the need for constant validation.

6. **Embrace Constructive Criticism:**
Constructive feedback is not about validation or approval—it's an opportunity for growth. Learn to distinguish between judgment and helpful feedback. When

you see criticism as a tool for improvement rather than a personal attack, you release the need for validation.

What Overcoming Needing Validation Will Allow You to Do

When you break free from the need for validation, you open the door to a range of empowering benefits:

- **Increased Confidence**: You will develop a strong, unwavering sense of self-worth that doesn't depend on others' opinions.
- **Freedom to Take Risks**: You will be more willing to take bold actions without fear of judgment or failure.
- **Authenticity**: You will be able to express yourself freely, without concern for how others perceive you.
- **Improved Relationships**: Free from people-pleasing, your relationships will become more genuine and fulfilling.
- **Sustained Motivation**: You will be driven by intrinsic motivation—your inner desire to grow, not the need for praise.

Breaking free from validation allows you to live more fully, with greater clarity, purpose, and resilience. Your worth is no longer defined by the opinions of others but by the confidence and belief you have in yourself.

Conclusion

Letting go of the need for external validation is not a one-time event; it's a continuous journey of self-discovery and growth. It takes conscious effort, practice, and a willingness to challenge the beliefs and habits that have shaped your life. But as you begin to rely more on your internal sense of worth, you will find that the freedom, clarity, and confidence you seek are already within you.

Call to Action

Are you ready to stop seeking validation and start living for yourself? Begin by setting one small goal today that is driven by your internal values, not external recognition. Reflect on your quiz results and commit to implementing one of the tools from this chapter. Take that first step toward breaking free from the cycle of validation—your true power lies within you.

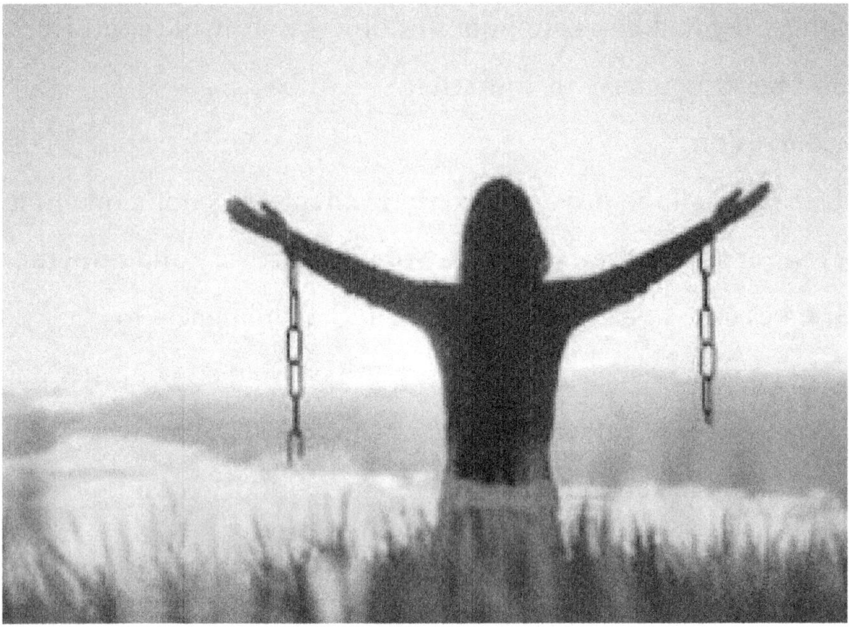

Chapter 12
Overcoming Lack of Self-Esteem

Introduction: Understanding Lack of Self-Esteem

Self-esteem is the foundation of how we see ourselves and the value we place on our abilities and worth. It impacts everything we do — from how we relate to others, to how we approach challenges, and even to how we perform at work. When self-esteem is low, it can hold us back from reaching our potential, leaving us feeling stuck, unworthy, and incapable.

Many men experience a lack of self-esteem at some point in their lives, often linked to societal pressures, personal setbacks, or unresolved internal struggles. When self-esteem takes a hit, it can result in feelings of inadequacy, self-doubt, and fear of failure. But the good news is that self-esteem is not fixed — it can be rebuilt and strengthened. In this chapter, we'll dive deep into the signs of low self-esteem, how it affects us, and most importantly, how to overcome it.

Lack of Self-Esteem in Action

Low self-esteem manifests in different ways, and understanding these behaviours is key to recognizing when it's impacting your life.

- **Negative Self-Talk**: The internal dialogue becomes critical and self-judging, constantly undermining your confidence and abilities. You might hear thoughts like "I'm not good enough" or "I'll never succeed."
- **Avoiding Challenges**: When you don't believe in your own abilities, you might shy away from opportunities that push you outside your comfort zone, fearing failure or rejection.
- **Difficulty Accepting Compliments**: If you don't value yourself, compliments from others can feel uncomfortable or even undeserved. You may downplay or dismiss positive feedback.
- **People-Pleasing**: A lack of self-esteem often leads to a tendency to please others in order to seek external

validation. This can leave you feeling drained and unfulfilled.
- **Procrastination**: Fear of not performing well enough or perfectionism can lead to putting things off. Low self-esteem breeds hesitation, making it harder to take action and make decisions.
- **Overthinking and Self-Doubt**: Constantly questioning your decisions or doubting your abilities can paralyze you and prevent forward movement.
- Recognizing these behaviours is the first step toward change. It's important to remember that these are just patterns — they can be unlearned, and better, healthier ones can take their place.

Interactive Quiz: Measure Your Level of Lack of Self-Esteem

Take a moment to reflect on the following questions. Answer them honestly on a scale from 1 to 5, with 1 = Never, 2 = Rarely, 3 = Sometimes, 4 = Often and 5 = Always.

1. I often doubt my abilities and feel unworthy of success.
2. I tend to avoid situations where I might fail or be judged.

3. I find it difficult to accept compliments from others.
4. I often feel that I need to please others to be accepted.
5. I frequently put off tasks due to fear of not performing well enough.
6. I compare myself to others and feel inferior.
7. I believe that I am not capable of achieving my goals.
8. I often feel that I am not enough, regardless of my achievements.
9. I find it hard to say "no" to others because I fear rejection.
10. I have trouble trusting my own decisions or judgment.

Scoring:

- 35-50 points: High level of low self-esteem. It's time to take action to rebuild your sense of self-worth.
- 20-34 points: Moderate low self-esteem. You may be struggling with certain aspects of your self-esteem, but you're aware of it and can make progress.
- 10-19 points: Low to moderate self-esteem. You have a solid foundation but may experience occasional self-doubt.
- 0-9 points: High self-esteem. You have a strong sense of self-worth, but it's always beneficial to maintain self-reflection and growth.

Tools to Overcome Lack of Self-Esteem

1. **Positive Affirmations**: Start each day by affirming your strengths and abilities. Write down statements like "I am enough," "I am worthy of success," and "I trust my judgment." Repeat them daily to retrain your mindset.
2. **Self-Compassion**: Treat yourself with kindness, especially when you make mistakes. Recognize that failure is part of the learning process and doesn't define your worth.
3. **Set Achievable Goals**: Start small. Set clear, manageable goals that challenge you without overwhelming you. As you achieve them, you'll build confidence in your abilities.
4. **Challenge Negative Self-Talk**: When you catch yourself thinking negatively, challenge those thoughts. Ask yourself, "Is this really true?" and replace the negative thought with a more balanced, empowering one.
5. **Surround Yourself with Positivity**: Spend time with people who uplift you, who encourage your growth, and who remind you of your strengths. Avoid those who bring you down or make you feel inferior.
6. **Practice Gratitude**: Take time each day to reflect on what you're grateful for, both in your personal and professional

life. Gratitude shifts your focus away from what you lack and highlights what you already have.
7. **Physical Activity**: Regular exercise can improve both physical and mental health, boosting your mood and energy levels while helping you feel more capable and stronger.
8. **Professional Support**: Consider seeking help from a coach or therapist who can guide you through the process of building self-esteem. Sometimes, having an outside perspective can offer valuable insights.

What Overcoming Lack of Self-Esteem Will Allow You to Do

When you rebuild your self-esteem, a whole new world opens up to you. Here's what you can expect:

- **Greater Confidence**: You'll trust your abilities and judgment, which will empower you to take on new challenges without fear.
- **Improved Relationships**: With better self-worth, you'll stop seeking validation from others and start forming more authentic, healthy relationships.

- **Increased Productivity**: As your self-esteem grows, you'll take action with confidence, overcoming procrastination and fear of failure.
- **Resilience in Adversity**: Strong self-esteem enables you to bounce back from setbacks, knowing that challenges don't define your worth.
- **A Clearer Path to Success**: With a positive mindset, you'll approach your goals with clarity and determination, knowing you deserve to succeed.
- By investing in yourself and your self-esteem, you unlock your potential to achieve anything you set your mind to.

Conclusion

Overcoming lack of self-esteem is a journey, but it's one that's entirely within your control. Recognizing the patterns that hold you back is the first step, and with the right tools and mindset, you can rewrite your story. You deserve to feel worthy, confident, and capable of achieving your dreams.

Call to Action

Take action today. Reflect on the quiz and identify where you can start implementing the tools shared in this chapter.

Write down three things you can do today to begin rebuilding your self-esteem. Whether it's a daily affirmation, a small goal, or seeking support, make a commitment to yourself. Your future self will thank you for it.

Remember: **You are worthy. You are capable. And you are enough.**

"You're allowed to assert your needs and take up space. You're allowed to hold onto the truth that who you are is exactly enough."

— Daniell Koepke

Chapter 13
Emotional Intelligence

Introduction

Emotional intelligence (EI) is the ability to recognize, understand, manage, and influence emotions—both your own and those of others. It's a key skill in navigating personal and professional relationships, improving decision-making, and maintaining mental well-being. While traditional intelligence (IQ) is about intellectual abilities and knowledge, emotional intelligence focuses on emotional skills and awareness. In today's fast-paced world, where stress, conflict, and uncertainty are common, emotional intelligence can be the differentiator that leads to success and fulfilment.

Unlike what many might think, emotional intelligence is not something you're either born with or without. It's a set of skills that can be developed and strengthened over time. Whether you're leading a team, building relationships, or trying to break through mental barriers, strengthening your EI can empower you to handle life's challenges with greater ease and confidence.

Emotional Intelligence in Action

Emotional intelligence is often divided into five key components, each of which plays a crucial role in our ability to interact effectively and manage emotions:

- **Self-Awareness:** The ability to recognize and understand your own emotions, strengths, weaknesses, and drives. Self-awareness allows you to see how your feelings influence your thoughts and behaviour, providing clarity in moments of stress or decision-making.
- **Self-Regulation:** This involves managing your emotions in a healthy way, controlling impulsive behaviours, and staying calm and clear-headed during challenging situations. It helps in responding to situations thoughtfully rather than reacting impulsively.
- **Motivation:** Emotionally intelligent individuals are driven by intrinsic goals and the desire to achieve personal growth and success. This internal motivation fuels resilience, persistence, and the pursuit of meaningful goals, even in the face of setbacks.
- **Empathy:** Empathy is the ability to understand and share the feelings of others. This goes beyond simply

recognizing emotional cues; it's about connecting with the emotions of others and responding appropriately to their needs.
- **Social Skills:** This includes the ability to manage relationships, communicate effectively, resolve conflicts, and work collaboratively. It is essential for building trust and fostering positive, productive interactions in both personal and professional settings.
- When you combine all of these components, you create a framework for navigating the emotional landscape of both your inner world and the world around you.

Interactive Quiz to Measure Your Level of Emotional Intelligence

Take a moment to reflect on the following questions to assess your emotional intelligence.

. Rate yourself on a scale of 1 to 5, with 1 = Never, 2 = Rarely, 3 = Sometimes, 4 = Often and 5 = Always.

1. I am aware of how my emotions impact my thoughts and behaviours.
2. I can stay calm and think clearly in stressful situations.

1. I am motivated by a desire for personal growth, not just external rewards.
2. I find it easy to understand how others are feeling, even without them saying anything.
3. I can communicate clearly and resolve conflicts effectively with others.
4. I am open to feedback and willing to make changes based on it.
5. I can easily adapt to changes in my environment or situation.
6. I am good at managing my emotional reactions, especially in difficult situations.

Scoring:

- **35-40 points**: High Emotional Intelligence. You have a strong grasp on managing your emotions and your relationships with others.
- **25-34 points**: Moderate Emotional Intelligence. There's room for growth, but you're on the right track.
- **Below 25 points**: Developing Emotional Intelligence. It's a great time to start actively working on your EI skills.
-

Tools to Support Growing Your Emotional Intelligence

1. **Mindfulness Practices:** Regular mindfulness exercises, such as deep breathing or meditation, can increase your self-awareness and improve your emotional regulation. By taking time to pause and tune into your emotions, you learn to respond more thoughtfully rather than react impulsively.
2. **Journaling:** Writing about your emotions helps to process and understand them more clearly. Journaling also provides a safe space to reflect on how your emotions influence your decisions, relationships, and actions.
3. **Active Listening:** Practice listening to others without interrupting or judging. Focus on understanding their perspective and emotions before responding. This builds empathy and strengthens relationships.
4. **Seeking Feedback:** Ask trusted friends, family members, or colleagues to provide constructive feedback on how you manage emotions and interact with others. Feedback is an essential tool for growth.

5. **Emotional Regulation Techniques:** Techniques like cognitive reframing (changing negative thoughts into positive ones), practicing self-compassion, and developing a support system are all essential for managing emotional responses.

What Developing Your Emotional Intelligence Will Allow You to Do

As you work to strengthen your emotional intelligence, the benefits will be vast and impactful in every area of your life:

- **Improved Decision-Making:** By understanding your emotions and how they influence your thoughts, you can make better, more objective decisions.
- **Enhanced Relationships:** With greater empathy and social skills, you will build stronger, more meaningful connections with others.
- **Increased Resilience:** Emotionally intelligent individuals can bounce back from setbacks more easily and adapt to change with greater flexibility.
- **Greater Leadership:** Whether you're leading a team or a family, strong emotional intelligence helps you inspire, guide, and motivate others with authenticity.

- **Mental Well-Being:** By managing stress, anxiety, and conflict with emotional intelligence, you'll find it easier to maintain a sense of peace and control over your emotions.

Conclusion

Emotional intelligence isn't a 'soft skill'—it's a powerful and essential tool that can shape every aspect of your life. By understanding your emotions, managing them effectively, and connecting with others on a deeper level, you unlock your full potential. Developing EI can transform your relationships, career, and overall well-being, making you a more resilient and effective individual in both your personal and professional spheres.

Call to Action

Take the first step toward improving your emotional intelligence today. Begin by committing to one of the tools listed above—whether it's journaling, practicing mindfulness, or seeking feedback. Reflect on your quiz results and choose an area you'd like to develop further. Remember, emotional intelligence is a skill you can grow, and each step you take will bring you closer to achieving your full potential.

Start small, stay consistent, and watch as you elevate your emotional intelligence to new heights

Chapter 14
Overcoming Perfectionism

Introduction

Perfectionism is often seen as a positive trait. It's associated with high standards, striving for excellence, and wanting the best outcomes. But beneath its polished surface, perfectionism can be a silent saboteur. It's the constant pressure to be flawless, the inner critic that never lets you settle, and the fear of making mistakes that paralyzes progress.

For professional men, perfectionism can be particularly damaging. It can hinder growth, erode confidence, and perpetuate a cycle of self-doubt and burnout. While striving for excellence can lead to success, perfectionism often causes unnecessary stress, delays, and missed opportunities. This chapter will explore the nature of perfectionism, how it manifests in everyday life, and most importantly, how to overcome it to achieve greater freedom, growth, and satisfaction in both your personal and professional life.

Perfectionism in Action

Perfectionism isn't always immediately noticeable. It often shows up in the following ways:

- **Procrastination:** The fear of not doing something perfectly can cause delays. You might avoid starting tasks because you're overwhelmed by the pressure to do them flawlessly.
- **Overworking:** Working longer hours and not taking breaks, pushing yourself beyond your limits to ensure everything is perfect, even at the expense of your well-being.
- **Self-Criticism:** After completing a task, the inner critic emerges, focusing on what went wrong rather than celebrating what was achieved. Nothing feels good enough.
- **Avoiding Feedback:** The fear of criticism or not meeting expectations leads you to avoid seeking constructive feedback from others. This can stunt your growth and isolate you from valuable opportunities for learning.
- **Impaired Relationships:** Perfectionism can strain relationships with colleagues, friends, and family. Your high standards might not be understood, and you may come across as demanding or hard to please.

- When perfectionism goes unchecked, it doesn't lead to better results—it leads to stress, burnout, and dissatisfaction. By recognizing perfectionism in action, you can begin to shift your mindset and take control over these behaviours.

-

Interactive Quiz: Measure Your Level of Perfectionism

1. Take a moment to reflect on the following statements. Rate yourself on a scale of 1 to 5, with 1 = Strongly disagree, 2 = Disagree, 3 = Neutral, 4 = Agree and 5 = Strongly Agree

2. I often delay tasks because I feel they need to be done perfectly.
3. I get frustrated when things don't go according to plan.
4. I often feel like my work isn't good enough, even when others compliment it.
5. I set unrealistically high standards for myself and others.
6. I avoid taking risks because I fear failure or making mistakes.
7. I feel a constant need to control every detail of a project.
8. I often overwork myself to make sure everything is perfect.

Scoring:

- 7-14: Low Perfectionism
- 15-21: Moderate Perfectionism
- 22-35: High Perfectionism

If your score is on the higher end, it may indicate that perfectionism is affecting your life in significant ways. This awareness is the first step in overcoming it.

Tools to Support Overcoming Perfectionism

Overcoming perfectionism is a process that involves shifting your mindset, managing your expectations, and embracing imperfection as a necessary part of growth. Here are some tools to support you in overcoming perfectionism:

1. **Set Realistic Expectations**: Understand that perfection is an unattainable standard. Instead, focus on doing your best while accepting that mistakes and imperfections are part of the process.
2. **Practice Self-Compassion**: Treat yourself with kindness, not judgment. Speak to yourself as you would to a friend who is struggling. Offer encouragement rather than criticism.
3. **Break Down Tasks**: Large tasks can be overwhelming. Break them into smaller, manageable steps to reduce the pressure of needing everything to be perfect from the start.
4. **Reframe Mistakes**: Instead of seeing mistakes as failures, view them as learning opportunities. Each mistake offers valuable insights that contribute to personal growth.
5. **Embrace "Good Enough"**: Adopt the concept of "good enough." Recognize that perfection is not always necessary for success, and sometimes "good enough" is all that's needed to move forward.
6. **Limit Time on Tasks**: Set time limits for each task to prevent you from obsessing over every detail. This

practice encourages efficiency and keeps you from getting bogged down by perfectionistic tendencies.
7. **Accountability Partner**: Find someone you trust to help hold you accountable. Share your goals and challenges with them and let them provide perspective on whether you're pushing yourself too hard.

What Overcoming Perfectionism Will Allow You to Do

When you start to let go of perfectionism, you create the space for greater freedom and personal growth. Here's what overcoming perfectionism will allow you to achieve:

- **Increased Productivity**: By focusing on progress over perfection, you'll get more done without overthinking every task.
- **Improved Confidence**: Embracing your flaws and imperfections will boost your self-esteem, as you begin to see your worth beyond flawless results.
- **More Time for What Matters**: By letting go of the need to be perfect, you free up time to focus on your passions, relationships, and personal development.

- **Less Stress**: Perfectionism often leads to stress and burnout. Letting go of this mindset will significantly reduce anxiety and mental exhaustion.
- **Enhanced Creativity**: With less pressure to perform flawlessly, you'll be more open to taking creative risks and exploring new ideas without fear of failure.
- **Stronger Relationships**: Allowing others to be imperfect and accepting your own imperfection fosters deeper, more authentic connections.

Conclusion

Perfectionism can be a powerful force in your life, but not always for good. It can hold you back, keep you from reaching your potential, and keep you trapped in a cycle of self-criticism and anxiety. However, overcoming perfectionism isn't about lowering standards—it's about being realistic, compassionate, and willing to embrace mistakes as a necessary part of success.

By recognizing perfectionism in your life, applying practical tools, and shifting your mindset, you'll unlock new levels of freedom, creativity, and personal growth. It's time to stop letting perfectionism dictate your actions and start embracing progress instead.

Call to Action

If you're ready to take the first step towards overcoming perfectionism, take a moment today to set a small, realistic goal. Whether it's starting a task without aiming for perfection or allowing yourself to make a mistake without judgment, commit to making progress.

Remember, overcoming perfectionism is a journey, not a destination. Each step you take brings you closer to the freedom of living a fulfilled, balanced, and authentic life.

Conclusion
Embrace Your Journey

As you've learned throughout this journey, the path to overcoming barriers like imposter syndrome, self-doubt, and anxiety is not a quick fix, but a continuous process of growth, self-discovery, and action. The tools, strategies, and insights shared here are not just theoretical—they are designed to empower you to make lasting changes in your life, starting right now.

Remember, your mindset is your most powerful tool. By shifting how you think, you unlock the ability to not only overcome challenges but to thrive in the face of them. The journey towards achieving your peak potential isn't about perfection; it's about progress. It's about confronting fears, embracing resilience, and developing a mindset that propels you forward.

Now, it's time to take the next step. The road ahead is yours to navigate, and you have everything you need to succeed. Keep applying the lessons you've learned here, reflect regularly on your growth, and be patient with yourself as you evolve into the person you are destined to become.

If you're ready to elevate your mindset and break through your barriers, know that you don't have to do it alone. The tools are available, and the support is there for you. Your peak potential is within reach, and it's waiting for you to claim it.

Elevate Your Mindset, Achieve Your Peak with Peak Mindset Coaching UK

If you're ready to take your mindset and personal growth to the next level, Peak Mindset Coaching UK is here to help. Through transformational coaching tailored to professional men, we focus on helping you break through the barriers that are holding you back—whether that's self-doubt, perfectionism, anxiety, or lack of confidence.

Get in touch today!
Email: peakmindsetcoachinguk@gmail.com
Phone: 07890094344

Book a **FREE Discovery Call** with me now, and let's discuss how you can start achieving your peak potential.

Together, we'll explore your challenges and set a clear, actionable path forward.

Printed in Great Britain
by Amazon